12 MUSICIANS
WHO CHANGED THE WORLD

by Jamie Kallio

L12

STORY LIBRARY

MORE TO EXPLORE

www.12StoryLibrary.com

12-Story Library is an imprint of Bookstaves.

Photographs ©: Chris Pizzello/Associated Press, cover, 1; Atlantic Records/PD, 4; Cecilio Ricardo/US Air Force, 5; Kathy Hutchins/Shutterstock.com, 5; Granamour Weems Collection/ Alamy, 6; Shanecollinswiki/CC3.0, 7; Ron Kroon/Anefo/PD, 8; Roland Godefroy/CC3.0, 9; Jaguar PS/Shutterstock.com, 10; DFree/Shutterstock.com, 11; Featureflash Photo Agency/ Shutterstock.com, 12; JStone/Shutterstock.com, 13; marcen27/CC2.0, 14; Comfurtn/ CC3.0, 15; ZUMA Press, Inc./Alamy, 16; Lenscap Photography/Shutterstock.com, 17; Pictorial Press Ltd/Alamy, 18; Tankfield/CC3.0, 19; Rowland Scherman/PD, 20; Christy Bowe/ Globe Photos/ZUMAPRESS.com/Alamy, 21; CBS Television/PD, 22; Bjoertvedt/CC4.0, 23; Ronincmc/CC4.0, 23; JStone/Shutterstock.com, 24; Pictorial Press/Alamy, 25; Globe Photos/ ZUMAPRESS.com/Alamy, 26; Kraft74/Shutterstock.com, 27; Tinseltown/Shutterstock.com, 28; lev radin/Shutterstock.com, 29; Kathy Hutchins/Shutterstock.com, 30

ISBN
9781632357182 (hardcover)
9781632358271 (paperback)
9781645820062 (ebook)

Library of Congress Control Number: 2019938662

Printed in the United States of America
July 2019

About the Cover
Aretha Franklin performing at the Nokia Theatre in 2012.

Access free, up-to-date content on this topic plus a full digital version of this book. Scan the QR code on page 31 or use your school's login at 12StoryLibrary.com.

Table of Contents

Aretha Franklin: Queen of Soul and Civil Rights

Aretha Franklin was a singer of gospel, jazz, R&B, and pop. A radio disc jockey nicknamed her the Queen of Soul. Franklin sang with expression and power. She would only perform songs that she connected to emotionally.

Born in Tennessee in 1942, Franklin was a child music prodigy. She had a strong voice and learned to play piano on her own. Her father was a civil rights activist and preacher. At the age of 10, Franklin sang gospel in his Detroit church. At 14, she recorded her first album.

Aretha Franklin in 1968.

In 1967, Franklin recorded "Respect," a song by Otis Redding. It became an anthem for civil rights. Franklin felt African Americans, women, and other marginalized people in America deserved respect. She used her music to help the civil rights movement. She funded activists by helping them travel. She even offered to post bail for activist Angela Davis when Davis was arrested. She was close friends with Dr. Martin Luther King Jr. and sang at his funeral in 1968.

Singers including Beyoncé and Jennifer Hudson were influenced by Franklin. Her legacy continues to attract new generations of listeners.

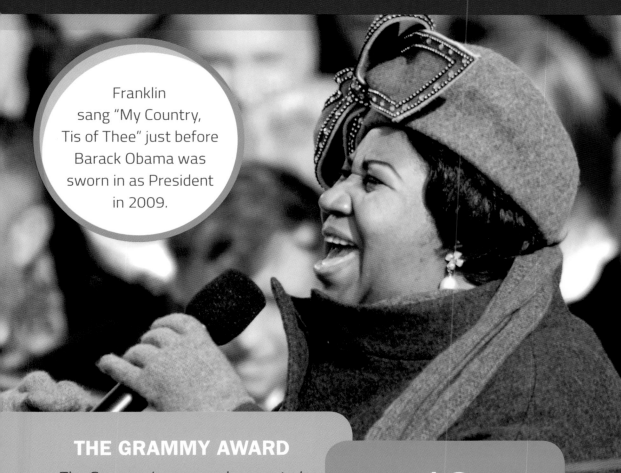

Franklin sang "My Country, Tis of Thee" just before Barack Obama was sworn in as President in 2009.

THE GRAMMY AWARD

The Grammy is an award presented by the Recording Academy, a society of music professionals. A Grammy is awarded to people who achieve excellence in the music industry. The first Grammy was given on May 4, 1959.

18
Number of Grammy awards Aretha Franklin won

- Franklin was nominated for 44 Grammys in her lifetime.
- She sold more than 75 million records worldwide.
- She was the first woman to be inducted into the Rock and Roll Hall of Fame.

Patsy Cline:
First Country Pop Star

Patsy Cline was one of the greatest singers in the history of country music. She was born Virginia Patterson Hensley in Virginia in 1922. At age eight, she taught herself to play piano. She was a talented singer. She performed on local radio stations and entered singing contests. A bandleader suggested she take Patsy as her stage name.

Cline signed a recording contract in 1954. Her first few songs were not popular. In 1957, she performed on the TV show *Arthur Godfrey's Talent Scouts*. She sang "Walkin' after Midnight" and won the prize. The song was both a country and pop hit. Her song "I Fall to Pieces" was on the music charts for 39 weeks. After this, she was labeled a pop singer. But Cline always considered herself a country singer.

Cline joined the Grand Ole Opry in Nashville, Tennessee, in the 1960s. She released some of her most famous hits during this time, including "Crazy." She toured with singers like Johnny Cash and June Carter. This was a time when male singers led the country music scene. Cline supported other women country singers.

In 1963, Cline died in a plane crash. In 1973, she became the first female artist elected to the Country Music Hall of Fame.

1947

Year of Patsy Cline's first radio performance

- Cline was one of the first country singers to have a crossover pop hit.
- Her hit song "Crazy" was written by singer Willie Nelson.
- She recorded "Crazy" on crutches after surviving a car crash.

In 1962, Cline was the first major country singer to perform in Las Vegas.

THE GRAND OLE OPRY

The Grand Ole Opry is a weekly live show in Nashville, Tennessee. It started as a radio show in 1925. The Opry has been called country music's most famous stage. It features a mix of performers. Some, like Dolly Parton, are country legends. Others, like Carrie Underwood, are contemporary musicians.

Nina Simone: She Put a Spell on Us

Nina Simone was born Eunice Kathleen Waymon in North Carolina in 1933. She started playing piano at age three. She played at her family's Methodist church. After high school, Simone attended the Juilliard School and studied classical music. She had to leave the school when she ran out of money.

In 1954, she began to perform in nightclubs. She sang and played jazz, blues, and folk music. She took the stage name Nina Simone. Soon she became well-known on the East Coast. In 1957, she signed a contract with Bethlehem Records. Her first album came out that year. Her song "I Loves You Porgy" became a Top 20 hit. Simone was called the High Priestess of Soul. She didn't like the nickname.

Simone wanted to use her music to change the lives of African Americans. She wrote many songs during the civil rights movement in the 1960s. Some were controversial, like "Four Women" and "To Be Young, Gifted and Black." Some of her music was banned from the radio in the South.

Simone traveled to many countries during her lifetime. She settled in France. For many years, she

Nina Simone in 1965.

didn't record
any music.
In the 1980s,
a perfume
commercial used her
song "My Baby Just Cares for
Me." This renewed her popularity.
In 1991, she published her
autobiography *I Put A Spell on You*.
Simone continued to sell
out shows when she toured.
When she died in France in
2003, hundreds of people
came to her funeral.

Simone
performing in
France in
1982.

THINK ABOUT IT

Why do you think Simone's songs
were banned from the radio in the
South? Try to find out.

40
Number of albums
Nina Simone made during
her lifetime

- Simone never had a
  No. 1 hit.
- She auditioned for
  the Curtis Institute of
  Music in Philadelphia
  but was rejected.
- She was friends with
  human rights activist
  Malcolm X.

Lady Gaga: Born This Way

Lady Gaga once wore a dress and ankle boots made of raw meat. She calls her fans Little Monsters. Her real name is Stefani Joanne Angelina Germanotta. She was born in New York in 1986 to an Italian American family. At age four, she learned to play piano. She took lessons in singing and acting. At 14, she gave her first performance at a New York City nightclub.

After high school, she attended the Tisch School of the Arts in New York. During this time, she created her stage persona. She took the name Lady Gaga after the Queen song "Radio Gaga." She modeled herself after glam artists like David Bowie. She wore flamboyant costumes. She became known for her music and her outfits.

In 2007, Gaga worked as a songwriter. She wrote songs for Britney Spears and Fergie. Her debut album, *The Fame*, came out in 2008. The first single released was "Just Dance." It reached No. 1 on the Billboard Pop Songs chart. Three more songs from *The Fame* became hits. The album sold more than 8 million copies. Gaga was nominated for five Grammys and won two.

Lady Gaga's controversial meat dress was meant as a statement for standing up for human rights.

Best song of the year "Shallow," from the movie *A Star Is Born*, earned Lady Gaga an Oscar in 2019.

2012
Year when Lady Gaga started her Born This Way Foundation

- Gaga uses her wealth and fame to help others.
- Her Born This Way Foundation works to support the wellness of young people and empower them to create a kinder world.
- Channel Kindness, launched in 2016, trains youth reporters to find, recognize, and report acts of kindness.

Lady Gaga has acted in several films and TV shows. In 2016, she won a Golden Globe Award for her performance in *American Horror Story: Hotel*. She starred in *A Star Is Born* in 2018. The movie earned more than $100 million in 12 days.

Mariah Carey: Songbird Supreme

New York City. She recorded a demo tape that made its way to Columbia Records. The label signed her in 1988.

Carey's first album, *Mariah Carey*, came out in 1990. The songs showed her vocal range and skill at different styles like gospel, pop, and R&B. Four No. 1 singles came from this album, including "I Don't Wanna Cry." In 1991,

Mariah Carey is known for singing high notes—higher than almost any other singer. She was born in New York in 1970. Her mother was a voice coach and opera singer. Carey started singing lessons at age four. She developed a voice that covered five octaves. After high school, she moved to

16

Number of weeks Mariah Carey's song "One Sweet Day" stayed on top of the Billboard charts

- So far, Carey has had 18 No. 1 songs.
- She has her own star on the Hollywood Walk of Fame.
- Carey is the 17th highest-selling artist of all time.

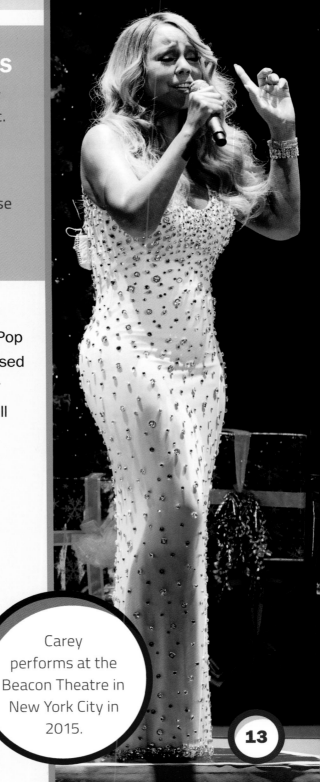

THE BILLBOARD CHARTS

Billboard magazine publishes many charts for different genres of music. Songs and albums make the charts based on sales, downloads, and radio play. Streaming services and social media are also included. These measurements are tracked all year long.

Carey won the Grammy awards for Best New Artist and Best Female Pop Vocalist. Over the years, she released 15 more albums. Carey shows her talent for singing many styles on all of her albums.

Carey is also an actress. In 2009, she won critical acclaim for her performance as a social worker in *Precious.* In 2012, she became a judge on the popular TV show *American Idol.* Carey is known for her humanitarian work. She helps raise money for the Make-a-Wish Foundation, which grants the wishes of children with life-threatening medical conditions.

Carey performs at the Beacon Theatre in New York City in 2015.

13

Adele: Old Soul

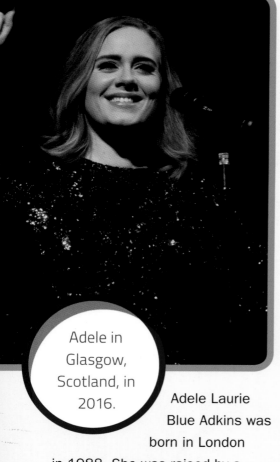

Adele in Glasgow, Scotland, in 2016.

Spice Girls and other pop music. Then she discovered singers like jazz star Ella Fitzgerald. The music inspired her throwback soulful sound.

Adele learned to play guitar and clarinet. The music program at her high school wasn't very good. At age 14, she was accepted to the BRIT School for Performing Arts and Technology. There, she had inspiring teachers. She learned how to write songs.

Adele recorded a demo for a class project. A friend posted it to the social media platform MySpace. Executives at XL Recordings heard the songs. They contacted Adele. In 2006, she signed a record deal. In 2008, she released her first album, *19*. She was 19 years old. Two of the album's songs, "Hometown Glory" and "Chasing Pavements," found fans in both Britain and the United States. Adele won two Grammys including Best New Artist.

Adele Laurie Blue Adkins was born in London in 1988. She was raised by a single mother. Her family was not musical, but she enjoyed singing. She listened to the

Adele performing at House of Blues in Cleveland, Ohio, in 2009.

In 2011, Adele's album, *21*, combined more classic R&B and jazz. It sold 352,000 copies in its first week. Two songs, "Rolling in the Deep" and "Someone Like You," were Top 5 hits in the same week.

Adele took some time off. She returned in 2015 with the album *25*. The album became an instant international hit. It reached No. 1 on iTunes in 100 countries. One of its most popular songs is the ballad "Hello." In 2017, Adele won five Grammys for *25*.

15
Number of Grammys Adele has won

- Adele has stage fright before every show.
- Her album *25* sold a million copies in the United Kingdom in 10 days.
- She won an Oscar in 2013 for writing the theme song for the James Bond movie *Skyfall*.

Prince: Nothing Compares 2 U

Prince performs on his Purple Rain tour in 1985.

Known as "The Purple One," Prince constantly reinvented himself. He influenced artists from Beck to Beyoncé. Born Prince Rogers Nelson in 1958 in Minneapolis, Minnesota, he grew up around music. His father was a pianist and songwriter. His mother was a jazz singer. Prince taught himself how to play

guitar, piano, and drums. He left high school at age 16.

In 1976, Prince worked as a studio guitarist in Minneapolis. He began to create the Minneapolis Sound, a blend of funk rock, synth-pop, and new wave. In 1977, he signed with Warner Records. He made a few albums that got attention. In 1982, his album *1999* was released. It topped the charts, and Prince became a regular on MTV videos. His signature look included his curly hair and ruffled shirts.

In 1984, Prince starred in the movie *Purple Rain*. It was based on his own life. He wrote and produced the soundtrack. Some of the songs include "Purple Rain" and "When Doves Cry." Prince won an Oscar for the soundtrack. Both the album and the movie were huge successes. The album sold more than 13 million

100 million

Number of records Prince sold worldwide before his death

- *Purple Rain* was No. 1 on the charts for 24 consecutive weeks.
- Prince won seven Grammy awards.
- He produced 39 studio albums.

SECRET HUMANITARIAN

Prince often gave secretly to charity. Some of his projects included Green for All, which creates green jobs for people in low-income communities. He also funded #YesWeCode to educate urban youth about technology.

copies. The film made over $70 million in the United States alone.

Prince was a prolific musician. He played different types of music such as jazz, funk, and R&B. He wrote hundreds of songs that were never released. Prince died from an accidental drug overdose in 2016. He was 57 at the time.

Prince was mourned world-wide after he died in 2016.

Bob Marley: One Love

Bob Marley in 1978.

single, "Simmer Down," topped the Jamaican charts. During the 1960s, the Wailers recorded for small Jamaican labels. Ska music was popular at the time. Marley became a Rastafarian. This was a political and religious movement that started in Jamaica. The Wailers signed with Island Records in the 1970s.

Bob Marley was a reggae legend. Almost four decades after his death, he is still a powerful influence on music, culture, politics, and fashion. Robert Nesta Marley was born in St. Ann Parish, Jamaica, in 1945. As a teen, he moved to Trench Town, a poor community that was also very musical. He learned to play guitar.

Marely recorded songs for a local record producer. He and two friends formed a band called Wailing Wailers. Their first

Marley wrote songs about political and social issues. His music changed from peppy ska to more mellow reggae. The Wailers helped to connect reggae with the rest of the world. Their songs like "One Love" and "No Woman, No Cry" have influenced other performers from hip-hop to rock, pop, and folk. Marley's message was about peace and tolerance. Once he earned money, he bought houses for friends in Jamaica. He would hand money to poor people waiting in line. Marley died of cancer in 1981. He was 36 years old.

50,000

Number of fans who attended Bob Marley's funeral in Jamaica National Arena

- Bob Marley and the Wailers never had a No. 1 Billboard chart hit while Marley was alive.
- Marley was posthumously awarded a Grammy Lifetime Achievement Award in 2001.
- *Legend*, a collection of Marley's songs released in 1984, is the best-selling reggae album in history.

Marley and the Wailers perform in 1980.

THINK ABOUT IT

Jamaica has been called a Third World country. Find out what that means. Do you think that term accurately describes Jamaica? Why or why not?

Bob Dylan: Voice of a Generation

Dylan performing during The Great March on Washington, DC in 1963.

2016

Year when Bob Dylan won the Nobel Prize in Literature

- He accepted his award at a private ceremony in a secret location.
- Dylan has won 10 Grammys, an Oscar, and a Golden Globe.
- He's a member of the Songwriters Hall of Fame and the Rock and Roll Hall of Fame.

countless musicians. He has created new genres of music.

Bob Dylan is the first songwriter to win the Nobel Prize for Literature. One of the most important individuals in the history pop culture, he has inspired

Born Robert Allen Zimmerman in 1941 in Minnesota, he learned to play guitar and harmonica when he was young. He listened to early rock stars like Elvis Presley. In high school, he formed a rock band called the Golden Chords. In college, he performed folk and country songs at cafés. He started calling himself Bob Dylan.

In 1960, Dylan moved to New York City. He played his music in folk clubs and coffeehouses. He wrote songs quickly, with a poetic style. He wrote about social justice issues and his romantic experiences. In 1961, he signed with Columbia Records. His first album, *Bob Dylan*, showed his writing talent and his gravel-voiced singing.

In 1962, he released *The Freewheelin' Bob Dylan*. One of the songs on the album was "Blowin' in the Wind." Dylan's 1965 album *Highway 61 Revisited* featured the song "Like A Rolling Stone." It's six minutes long. Until that time, radio stations wouldn't play songs over three minutes. When Dylan switched from acoustic guitar to electric guitar, he invented folk-rock. His memoir, *Chronicles: Volume One*, was a national best seller.

THINK ABOUT IT

Is there a social justice issue you care deeply about? What would you like to say? Brainstorm some ideas. Try writing a song or poem.

Elvis Presley: The King of Rock and Roll

Elvis Aron Presley was born in Tupelo, Mississippi, in 1935. His family was poor. Elvis started singing with his church choir as a child. He got his first guitar as a birthday present when he was 12 and taught himself how to play. When he was 13, the family moved to Memphis.

After graduating from high school in 1953, Elvis cut a demo record at Sun Studio. His first single, "That's All Right," was released in 1954. The song was a type of blues, but Elvis's voice and singing style changed the sound. He had invented rockabilly.

In January 1956, Elvis signed with RCA Records. He released the song "Heartbreak Hotel." It reached No. 1 on the charts and stayed there for seven weeks. Elvis signed a movie contract with Paramount Pictures. With his slick hair and swinging hips,

Elvis Presley in 1956.

Elvis made an impression. Critics said he was a bad influence on young people. But Elvis was polite when he gave interviews. His music let young people express themselves.

Elvis died in 1976 at age 42. He and his music cemented the popularity of rock and roll. He inspired many musicians such as Jerry Lee Lewis, John Lennon, and Bruce Springsteen. Elvis is still one of the world's most famous icons.

Graceland, and the Jungle Room, where Elvis recorded much of his last two albums before his death.

GRACELAND

In 1957, Elvis bought Graceland, a mansion in Memphis. He made many changes to the mansion, such as adding the Jungle Room with its indoor waterfall. Graceland is now open to the public. Fans from around the world visit, especially around the anniversary of his death.

$4.00
What Elvis paid to record the song "My Happiness," a gift for his mother

- He had a twin brother named Jesse who died shortly after birth.
- His first million-selling record, "Heartbreak Hotel," came out in 1956.
- In 1957, Elvis was famously drafted into the United States Army.

David Bowie: The Chameleon

David Bowie performs in New York in 2003.

David Bowie shaped musical genres and opened minds. He was born David Robert Jones in London in 1947. At age 13, he learned to play saxophone.

After graduating from high school, Bowie led a group called Davy Jones and the Lower Third. But he didn't want to be confused with Davy Jones from the Monkees, another band popular at the time. So he took the last name Bowie, after the Bowie knife.

In 1969, Bowie signed with Mercury Records. His first song was "Space Oddity." It was inspired by the film *2001: A Space Odyssey*. The British Broadcasting System (BBC) used it to cover the Apollo 11 moon landing. Bowie followed with the albums *The Man Who Sold the World* in 1970 and *Hunky Dory* in 1971.

Bowie's style changed often. Sometimes his music was folk-rock. Other times, it was pop or electronic. He experimented with fashion. He created different characters to go with his music, such as Ziggy Stardust and the Thin

White Duke. He kept audiences guessing. Bowie was also an actor. In 1976, he starred in the movie *The Man Who Fell to Earth*. In 1986, he played the Goblin King in the fantasy film *Labyrinth*.

Bowie's music career spanned 50 years. Many of his songs, such as "Let's Dance" and "China Girl," are still popular. He inspired fans to take their own creative risks. Bowie was concerned with social issues. He challenged gender roles. He spoke against political corruption in songs like "Changes" and "Heroes." In 1996, Bowie was inducted into the Rock and Roll Hall of Fame. He released his final album, *Blackstar*, on his 69th birthday in 2016. He died two days later.

2006

Year when David Bowie received the Grammy Lifetime Achievement Award

- Bowie made 27 studio albums during his lifetime.
- He acted in 27 films.
- He sold an estimated 140 million records.

Bowie in 1974.

Tupac Shakur: Poet from the Streets

Tupac Shakur was born Lesane Parish Crooks in East Harlem, New York, in 1971. His parents were involved with the Black Panthers. When he was two years old, his mother renamed him Tupac Amaru Shakur, after an 18th-century revolutionary.

As a teenager, Shakur studied at the Baltimore School for the Arts. He won many rap competitions. Before he could graduate, he and his mother moved to California. Shakur spent time on the streets and got involved with gangs.

In 1990, he joined the rap group Digital Underground. In 1991, he released his debut album, *2Pacalypse Now*. It contained the controversial song "Brenda's Got a Baby." The lyrics set off talks about race and street violence. In 1995, Shakur signed with Death Row Records. A year later, his double album *All Eyez on Me* came out. The song "California Love" went to No. 1 on the Billboard Hot 100 chart. The album sold more than 10 million copies in its first year. Shakur acted in several films, including *Juice*

Tupac Shakur in 1994.

75 million

Number of Tupac Shakur records sold, many after his death

- At 13, Shakur acted in the play *A Raisin in the Sun* at the Apollo Theater in Harlem.
- He was a fan of William Shakespeare.
- Shakur's song "Dear Mama" is in the Library of Congress.

THE BLACK PANTHERS

The Black Panther Party was created in 1966 in Oakland, California. The group wanted to monitor police activity in black neighborhoods. They stood for black pride and civil rights. They started social programs to help black people find jobs and good housing. The Black Panthers disbanded in 1982.

in 1991, *Poetic Justice* in 1993, and *Bullet* in 1996.

Shakur's personal life grew more troubled. In 1996, when he was 25, he was killed in a drive-by shooting. The shooter was never caught. A book of Shakur's poetry, *The Rose That Grew from Concrete*, was published in 2000.

More Musicians to Know

Taylor Swift: Crossover Sensation

Taylor Swift was born in Pennsylvania in 1989. She began writing her own songs and playing guitar at age 12. Swift broke into country music at age 16. Her first single, "Tim McGraw," spent eight months on the Billboard country charts. Her 2008 album, *Fearless*, crossed over into pop. Swift has won hundreds of awards and sold tens of millions of albums. Her video views are in the billions.

Kelly Clarkson: Idol Winner

Kelly Clarkson was born in 1982 in Fort Worth, Texas. Growing up, she had a powerful voice. In 2002, a friend told her about a new show on Fox called *American Idol*. Clarkson was the first winner. Her prize was $1 million and a record contract with RCA. Her first song, "A Moment Like This," reached No. 1 on the Billboard charts. Clarkson has been nominated for 15 Grammys and won three.

Kelly Clarkson at the 2019 Billboard Music Awards.

Michael Jackson: King of Pop

Michael Jackson was born into a musical family in 1958 in Gary, Indiana. When he was six, he started his music career with his brothers. They were called the Jackson Five and produced four No. 1 hit singles. Jackson started a solo career in the late 1970s. Albums like *Thriller* made him a superstar. On February 28, 1984, Jackson won eight Grammys on one night. He was famous for his dance moves, including the moonwalk.

Lin-Manuel Miranda: Hip-Hop on Broadway

Lin-Manuel Miranda was born in 1980 to Puerto Rican parents. He is best known for his musical *Hamilton*. Miranda came up with the idea after reading a biography of Alexander Hamilton, one of the Founding Fathers of the United States. The musical blends hip-hop and other styles of music. *Hamilton* was nominated for 16 Tony awards, Broadway's biggest honor. It won 11 including Best Musical. Miranda also won a Grammy for writing the song "How Far I'll Go" for the 2016 Disney movie *Moana*.

Lin-Manuel Miranda in 2019.

Glossary

controversial
To cause disagreement.

flamboyant
Something or someone that is colorful or eye-catching.

genre
A type or category of art or literature.

glam
Flashy or showy.

icon
An important symbol of a time or culture.

marginalized
Considered unimportant or ignored.

octave
A series of eight notes in a musical scale.

posthumously
Something that happens after a person's death.

prodigy
Someone who has a natural talent or ability.

prolific
Productive; creative.

Read More

Berman, Kathleen Cornell. *Birth of the Cool: How Jazz Great Miles Davis Found His Sound*. Salem, MA: Page Street Publishing, 2019.

O'Connor, Jim. *What Is Rock and Roll?* New York: Penguin Workshop, 2017.

Yacka, Douglas, and Francesco Sedita. *Where Is Broadway?* New York: Penguin Workshop, 2019.

Visit 12StoryLibrary.com

Scan the code or use your school's login at **12StoryLibrary.com** for recent updates about this topic and a full digital version of this book. Enjoy free access to:

- Digital ebook
- Breaking news updates
- Live content feeds
- Videos, interactive maps, and graphics
- Additional web resources

Note to educators: Visit 12StoryLibrary.com/register to sign up for free premium website access. Enjoy live content plus a full digital version of every 12-Story Library book you own for every student at your school.

Index

About the Author

Jamie Kallio is the author of many nonfiction children's books. She is a librarian in the south suburbs of Chicago. She can play piano by ear.